a t
or t
about™

Baseball

by **David Fischer**

Rick Wolff, Series Editor

**a thing
or two
media**™
WESTPORT, CT

To Rachel and Jack, who make their Big Coach proud.

Design: Fabia Wargin Design
Editor: Matt Levine
Proofreader: Sue J. Lowe
Cartoonist: Ron Zalme
Icon Artist: Chris Reed
Technique Diagrams: Rolin Graphics
Photo Credits:
    SW Production/Index Stock Imagery: 9
    Corbis Images: 13
    PhotoDisc: 22, 25, 31, 62
    © Image Club Graphics: 26, 29, 49
    AP/Wide World Photos: 30, 52, 57, 61, 78, 81, 83, 84, 85
    Bob Jacobson/Index Stock Imagery: 45
    Zephyr Picture/Index Stock Imagery: 49

TABLE OF CONTENTS

Let me clue you in on a little secret when it comes to baseball.

Baseball is a very difficult sport to play—especially when you're only a kid and you haven't really played it before. Unlike soccer, where just about everybody can learn how to kick a soccer ball, or basketball, where just about everybody can learn how to dribble and shoot the ball, baseball is a sport that involves all kinds of unique challenges: First, kids have to learn how to throw a ball. Then they have to learn how to catch one. Then they must learn how to hit a baseball with a bat—and on and on.

Furthermore, eager parents who want their kids to shine as Little Leaguers often forget that even the best big league stars routinely strike out, make errors, give up home runs, miss popups, and so forth. Even the best pro hitters fail to get a hit seven times out of ten, and many pitchers sport a .500 record or lower.

So you see, Mom and Dad, since it is agreed that baseball is a very difficult sport to play well, *please* keep that basic premise in mind when you start your little slugger in youth league baseball. Yes, it's frustrating, irksome, quirky, and at times, disappointing. But that's the nature of baseball, and according to many, it's still the greatest game ever invented.

But what do you say to your youngster when he strikes out with the bases loaded? Or she walks six batters in a row? Or you are asked to explain a force play?

Relax! This is where *A Thing or Two about Baseball* can save the day. In this volume, you will find lots of inspirational stories of famous Major Leaguers who have struggled with the game of baseball over the years. You'll also find the basic rules of the sport explained. And you'll find lots of time-tested suggestions on how to handle those delicate conversations with your children when they become a bit frustrated by the game. Of course, there's also plenty of solid advice on everything from how to select the right size bat for your slugger to how to teach all of the basic skills.

A Thing or Two about Baseball is the perfect primer to guide you through the ups and downs of any youth league baseball season. It will always keep you and your youngsters on the right track in your ongoing attempt to improve their baseball skills. Best of all, like the game itself, *A Thing or Two about Baseball* is designed to be fun.

RICK WOLFF, Series Editor
February 2001

How to Use This Book

Of all the reasons why parents want their children to play baseball, the most important reason is to have fun. However, young athletes are often overwhelmed by frustrations during early sports experiences. Baseball in particular is a difficult game to play, and its rules are not always easy to understand. That's where *A Thing or Two about Baseball* comes in handy.

This book is intended for parents who want to help their children, ages 5 to 12, learn the basics of baseball. It will help you and your child overcome the obstacles and experience the pleasures of participating in an organized youth baseball league. In this book, you'll learn basic baseball rules and strategies and how to apply them so that you and your young athlete will get the most from the game. You'll discover some easy backyard drills that will help your child improve his or her skills; and you'll find tips for being a positive sports parent, dealing with winning and losing, and communicating with your child's coach. Health and safety issues will also be discussed. The book contains valuable resources and references, a section of frequently asked questions—plus a whole lot more.

START AT SQUARE ONE

Think back to when you were a kid, and baseball was a new experience. Remember the frustration you felt trying to throw, catch, and hit? That's what your child is feeling now. So put yourself in your child's shoes. Have a catch with your youngster while wearing a glove on the wrong hand, and try to throw the ball accurately with your opposite hand. If you're right-handed, try batting left-handed for a change. This brief experiment will remind you of the difficulty of playing baseball and will provide some comic relief for both you and your child.

■ Play Ball!

Most kids at least consider playing organized baseball at some point during their elementary school years. The old-time sandlot games, however, are long gone. Today, parents worry about whether participation in organized sports will be good for their children. Will the pressures to compete outweigh the benefits of teamwork and exercise that sports offer? Will the coach be sensitive to their children's needs, or will he or she insist on winning at any cost? Will out-of-control parents spoil the experience for themselves and their children? Will practices and games interfere with other pursuits, especially school? If you are one of these parents, this book will help you and your child get the most from organized youth baseball.

The truth is that playing baseball is still a great experience for thousands of kids and their parents. The benefits of socializing with friends, learning and developing skills, being part of a team— not to mention just getting out in the fresh air and playing—are all still part of youth league baseball. As long as both kids and parents keep their priorities straight, organized youth baseball can be a great, positive experience for everyone. The key to having fun is simple: Keep the emphasis on playing the game and becoming a better player by the end of the baseball season rather than on wins and losses.

Should your child play youth baseball? Only you can answer that question. It takes patience, persistence, and a good measure of determination to become a good baseball player. But most kids know the secret to having fun with the game: Just play ball! By the time you finish this book, you'll know the secrets to making that formula work for your child.

IS THAT A FACT?

Although there are other youth leagues, Little League Baseball, established in 1939, is the largest and best-known organized baseball program for kids. Today, more than three million children, ages 8 to 12, in over 90 countries, play Little League Baseball. Other popular youth leagues include Police Athletic Leagues, Pony Baseball, the National Amateur Baseball Federation, the Babe Ruth League, T-Ball, and Dixie Baseball, to name a few. See Chapter 8 for a more complete listing.

REAL-LIFE EXAMPLES

DEREK JETER, the All-Star shortstop of the New York Yankees, suffered through a horrible first season in the minor leagues. Drafted out of high school as the number 6 pick in the nation in 1992, Jeter managed just a .202 batting average. In 1993, Derek made 56 errors—the third-highest total in the minors that season.

CHIPPER JONES also found success after a rough start. The first overall selection in the 1990 draft, Jones hit a paltry .229 with only one home run. He made 18 errors in 44 games. In spite of his slow start, Chipper soon became a dominant force in the National League. He lead the Atlanta Braves to the 1995 World Series title and then won the Most Valuable Player award in 1999.

■ Danger: Kids at Play

One of the serious concerns that many parents have about organized youth leagues is that they tend to focus on the results of competition, rather than the enjoyment of spontaneous and creative play. Youth baseball will be a lot more fun if your child's self-esteem does not depend on performance in the game. Reinforce the fact that you love your child and are proud of him or her regardless of how well he or she plays.

As a parent, fight the urge to compare your child's athletic ability with that of other kids on the team. Don't worry where your child's skills rank compared with those of his or her teammates. Instead, focus on whether he or she is having a good time. Kids mature at different speeds, and their skill levels develop at varying rates. Remember, athletic ability at an early age often has little bearing on future athletic success. Keep the emphasis on fun and participation, not achievement.

■ Ready, Set, Play!

Is your child emotionally ready to experience organized baseball? More than anyone else, you know your child's capabilities, and if you're reading this book, you probably feel your child is ready to play ball. Here are a few things to keep in mind as you ponder that first big plunge into organized sports.

It's great for parents to encourage their children to participate in organized sports, but be wary of crossing the line between encouraging and pressuring. If your child seems reluctant to join a league, discuss the reasons why. Don't push your goals on him or her. No matter how much you want your child to play, if he or she is not self-motivated, the experience will not be positive. It's always best to let the child figure out his or her ideal degree of commitment to baseball without undue pressure.

Keep in mind that playing baseball should not consume all of your child's time. If your child chooses to play, set realistic boundaries and expectations. Be clear that you won't allow baseball to get in the way of other important pursuits—like music lessons! Be certain your young athlete makes time to do schoolwork and discovers a variety of hobbies. In the long run, your child is much more likely to stay with the game if baseball is one element of a well-rounded group of activities. For an 8-year-old, two or three hour-long practices a week and one or two games a week is a sensible schedule. The entire baseball season should last about two to three months. As age, skill level, and fitness increase, so, too, can the length and frequency of practices and games.

■ Personal Goals

Often, winning a baseball game depends on factors out of any single player's control. These include the performance of teammates and opponents, umpires' decisions, and pure luck. Instead of focusing on winning and losing, encourage your child to strive for personal goals— fielding ground balls correctly, hitting the ball sharply, or throwing on target to a base. Offer support, and help him or her develop a personal yardstick for measuring achievement that isn't influenced by such external factors as peer pressure and competitive environment. Discuss the child's goals with him or her before each game or practice. If these goals are realistic, your child will experience more success and feel more competent. In addition, achieving realistic goals will help foster the confidence to learn more difficult skills without the fear of failure. When success is defined as exceeding personal goals instead of doing better than others, winning or losing becomes secondary.

MORE THAN A GAME

Many studies have shown that children who participate in sports do better academically. This is no great surprise to most parents. Many of the skills required to play baseball translate into good study habits. Children learn to be disciplined, and they learn to organize their time more effectively. These are extremely important tools in planning proper time for homework, projects, and other school activities. In addition, kids who play sports are more likely to stay in school and stay off drugs. Will baseball make your son or daughter a better student? Not by itself. But organized baseball can be an important part of any well-rounded student's daily life.

REAL-LIFE EXAMPLE

Some say Colorado Rockies superstar LARRY WALKER is a natural talent. The two-time National League batting champion and 1997 Most Valuable Player certainly makes the game look easy. But Walker's high school didn't have a baseball team, and he had a tough time learning the rules of baseball. As a minor leaguer, Larry once ran from first base to third before realizing that the batter had flied out. Larry didn't know that he had to touch second base on his way back to first, so he ran across the infield and was called out. "That tells you how far you can come in this game," now says Walker, who had phoned his father, wanting to quit.

■ Why Kids Quit

Even children who start their baseball careers with enthusiasm can change their minds. If your child seems to have lost interest or says he or she wants to quit the team, ask if he or she is still having fun playing baseball and listen carefully to the answers. This is a time to keep your desires out of the picture. You may want your child to continue, but resist the urge to pressure him or her. Don't try to change the child's mind by appealing to his or her commitment to the team. Children under 8 often don't understand this concept.

Kids have as many reasons for quitting baseball as they have for playing. Younger children may want to quit because they are afraid of being hit by the ball. No problem. Safety balls, called *reduced-impact* or *sting-free balls,* are available from the Jugs Company and should lessen the fear factor (see Chapter 8). Other children may want to quit baseball because their interests have changed, or because they lack playing time or fear failure. Some kids feel psychological stress caused by a coach with a "win-at-all-costs" mentality. Older kids may simply have lost interest or want to move on to new experiences and a new peer group. Whatever the reason, quitting baseball should not necessarily be seen as negative. If signs of disinterest persist over a period of time, you may want to reconsider whether playing organized baseball is right for your child.

It's healthy for children of all ages to sample many different activities, including several sports, before deciding which ones they want to pursue. Quitting baseball in order to concentrate on piano lessons or soccer is an admirable decision. Psychologists grow concerned, however, when kids quit because their self-worth is threatened through repeated failure or when they feel stressed out by criticism. Parents and coaches should be sensitive to these issues and should ensure that baseball enhances a child's self-worth rather than diminishing it. As a parent, try to understand your child's reasons for wanting to quit. If there is a problem that can be solved, then tackle it. However, if your child is determined to move on, talk it over and make the decision together. Remember, there is always next season.

Even if your child quits or takes a season off, it may not be the end of his or her baseball career, especially if another sport is taken up. The majority of professional players did not grow up as one-sport specialists. Few children—even those who exhibit a lot of talent—have the natural desire or dedication to practice baseball and only baseball. Children whose lives are built around a single sport tend to burn out on that sport. In addition, they miss out on the benefits that other sports offer. Consequently, single-sport kids often resent not only the sport, but also the adults who pressured them to play. This is especially true when a child plays the same sport all year. Spring baseball, followed by baseball summer camp, followed by autumn ball, followed by winter clinics can be too much. Taking some time off from baseball to pursue other things may renew your child's interest when next season rolls around.

TWO-SPORT STARS

★★ Cleveland Indians outfielder **KENNY LOFTON** played guard on his University of Arizona college basketball team, which reached the Final Four.

★★ Pitcher **TOM GLAVINE** of the Atlanta Braves was an exceptional high school hockey player who was drafted by the National Hockey League's Los Angeles Kings.

★★ California Angels outfielder **DARIN ERSTAD** was a two-sport star in college at Nebraska. In addition to playing baseball, he was the punter on the Cornhuskers' national championship football squad.

■ Summing Things Up

Baseball provides terrific lessons, and it's fun for kids to play and be part of a team. Just keep these guidelines in mind so you and your child have a great time.

- Keep the emphasis on fun and play—not winning and losing.
- Set personal goals, and help your child measure his or her progress against these rather than outside influences.
- Encourage but don't pressure.
- Keep baseball in perspective—get involved in other activities.
- When baseball stops being fun, it's probably time to take a break.

■ The Object of the Game

If you're new to the game, every-thing you need to know to help your child and to get more enjoyment from watching him or her play is spelled out here. If you know the game, reading through the basic rules may refresh your memory or give you a new bit of information.

Youth leagues follow the same basic rules as the majors. However, there are many variations on the rules designed to make the game more playable and safer for young players. We've noted many such variations below. Check your league's rules to see how they may vary from the basics.

Please note that the rules explained in this chapter have been simplified. Baseball is a complicated game with many variables, and there are numerous exceptions to the rules. Don't worry—you'll learn the exceptions as you watch your child play. In the meantime, at least you'll know the basics. Definitions of baseball terms and more detailed references can be found at the back of this book.

Let's start at the beginning. In baseball, there are nine players on a team. Two teams take turns playing offense and defense. When a team plays offense, the goal is to travel around the *bases* and score *runs*. When a team plays defense, the goal is to get the other team's players *out*, preventing them from scoring runs. The team that scores the most runs by the end of the game is the winner.

■ The Playing Field

A baseball field is made up of the *infield*—the part of the field close to home plate that contains the bases—and the *outfield*, which is usually a large grassy area beyond the infield. The infield is often called a *diamond*, because it is a square turned at an angle with a base located at each corner. *Home plate* is where a player must start and end a trip around the bases. In order, from right to left, the bases are *first base*, *second base*, and *third base*. The distance between the bases on a big league field is always 90 feet. Youth fields are two-thirds the size of big league diamonds, which places the bases 60 feet apart. The part of the field within the *baselines* (lines running from home plate to first and third bases) is called *fair territory*. Outside of the baselines is considered *foul territory*.

■ Beginning a Game

To start a game, a *batter* (an offensive player) stands at home plate with a bat.

A player in the field called a *pitcher* tries to throw the baseball over home plate within a certain area called the *strike zone*. Major league rules define the width of the strike zone as the area over any part of home plate. The area from the batter's armpits to his or her knees defines the height of the strike zone.

The batter's goal is to get on base. This can be accomplished in three ways. The first is to use the bat to hit a pitch into fair territory and safely run to a base. The second is to be hit by a pitch—this automatically results in a free trip to first base for the batter. The last way to reach base is to be *walked* by the pitcher.

Any pitch that passes through the strike zone is called a *strike*. Any pitch at which a batter swings and misses is also a strike. And any pitch which the batter hits into foul territory is a strike. Any pitch outside the strike zone at which a batter does not swing is called a *ball*. If a batter gets four balls, he or she gets a walk, which is a free trip to first base. If a batter gets three strikes, he or she is out. This is called a *strikeout*. However, the batter cannot be struck out by hitting a pitch into foul territory when he or she already has two strikes. The batter may hit any number of fouls.

■ The Offense

The batter's objective when swinging the bat is to hit the pitch into fair territory and away from the players on the field (fielders). Once the batter hits into fair territory, he or she must drop the bat and run for first base. If he or she thinks it is safe, the batter may try to advance farther—to second or third base. A one-base hit is called a *single*, a two-base hit is a *double*, and a three-base hit is a *triple*. A four-base hit is a *home run*. A home run most often occurs when a ball is hit out of the playing field while still in fair territory.

Hit balls are often categorized in three basic ways: *groundballs*, *line drives*, and *fly balls*. A groundball, or *grounder*, is a ball hit on the ground. A line drive is a ball hit in the air straight out from the bat. A fly ball, or *popup*, is a ball hit high in the air. If a line drive or a fly ball is caught in the air, the batter is out.

A batter who safely reaches base becomes a *base runner*. A base runner may advance if the next batter hits a fair ball. A base runner on first base must run toward second base when the batter hits a groundball. When the bases are loaded (players on all three bases), all of the base runners have to run when the batter hits a grounder. When a base runner must run, the play is called a *force play*, because the runner is forced to try to advance to the next base. When a player makes it safely around all the bases and touches home plate, he or she scores a run for the team.

This young player slides in for a stolen base.

In a major league game, a base runner may also advance when the batter does not hit the pitch. If the runner reaches the base successfully, it's called a *stolen base*. But the runner can be put out if the catcher throws the ball to an infielder who *tags* him or her (touches him or her with the ball) before the runner reaches the base. Little League rules do not allow stolen bases. However, some youth leagues for older kids do allow base stealing.

■ The Defense

A Little League baseball game consists of six *innings*. (Extra innings may be played if the score is tied at the end of the sixth inning.) One inning is completed when each team has a turn at bat. Each team's time at bat is regarded as a *half-inning*. A half-inning is completed when the fielding team gets three opposing players out.

In the field, the pitcher stands on the *pitcher's mound*, a small mound in the center of the infield. On top of the mound is the *pitcher's rubber*, a slab of rubber on which the pitcher must stand when throwing pitches. In major league games, the pitcher's rubber is always 60 feet, 6 inches from home plate, but in Little League, the pitcher's rubber is 46 feet away from the plate.

In addition to the pitcher, the fielding team has five other players positioned in the infield. The *catcher* stands or squats behind home

See the diagram on the inside back cover.

plate and receives the pitches thrown by the pitcher. Any pitch that makes it past the batter should be caught by the catcher and thrown back to the pitcher for the next pitch. Around the infield are positioned the *first baseman*, *second baseman*, *shortstop*, and *third baseman*. The shortstop occupies the space between second and third base, while the second baseman is positioned between second and first base. In the outfield are the *right fielder*, *center fielder*, and *left fielder*.

■ Outs

There are several ways the fielding team can get the players at bat out. One is to have a pitcher strike out a batter, throwing three strikes before the batter hits the ball or is issued a walk.

If any batted ball is caught by a fielder before it touches the ground, the batter is out. This is true whether the ball is in fair or foul territory.

To make an out on a force play, a fielder must either field the ball (catch a ball hit by the batter) him- or herself or receive a fielded ball from a teammate and put one foot on the base before the runner gets there. This is true of any play made to first base.

A player on second base does not have to run if a ball is batted while first base is unoccupied. Nor does a player on third base have to run unless both first and second are occupied. Should a player run when not forced, a fielder can tag the runner out by touching him or her with the ball or the glove while holding the ball in it. However, the player will not be out if the fielder only steps on the next base while holding the ball. A player may actually be tagged out at any time that he or she is off a base.

When a line drive or fly ball is caught for an out, all runners must return to the bases they previously occupied. If the ball arrives at a base before the runner gets back, he or she is out. But it is possible to advance to a vacant base or to score a run from third base on a fly ball by *tagging up*. This means standing on the base until after the catch has been made and then running to the next base before the ball arrives there. A runner who has tagged up must be tagged out and is not subject to a *force play*.

Equipment

Baseball is played with a *ball* and a *bat*. Each player also needs a *fielder's glove* to catch the ball. On the field, there are *bases*, which are square canvas bags (15 inches on a side) filled with sand or sawdust. Home plate is a rubber slab with five sides. Each side is 17 inches.

Baseballs are made of two pieces of cowhide stitched together over a ball of tightly wound yarn. At the center is a small, round cork coated with rubber. A baseball weighs about 5 ounces and is about 9 inches around.

■ Bats

Bats, which are used by batters to make contact with pitched balls, are usually made out of wood from northern white ash trees. Metal bats made of aluminum are also common in youth leagues, but they are not allowed in the major leagues. This is because balls hit with aluminum bats can travel so hard and fast that pitchers would be in danger of being struck by such balls before they could protect themselves. Because kids hit the ball with much less force than major leaguers do, aluminum bats are safe for youth baseball.

Most professional players now use light bats that weigh about 33 ounces to maintain bat speed, which is the top priority in hitting. Youngsters use bats that are significantly smaller. However, it's still crucial that an inexperienced player have a light bat to swing. This gives a player enough bat speed to hit the ball with authority. According to Louisville Slugger bat engineer George Manning, "A starting player needs to learn to make contact with the ball and hit close to the 'sweet spot' of the bat before performance differences in the bats become an important factor."

Most organized leagues supply each team with a number of bats. When your child selects a bat, it's better to pick one that is too short or too light than too heavy or too long. The bat's handle, or *grip*, should not be too wide. Remember: A thinner handle provides increased bat speed. A player should be able to handle a bat that can be held straight out in front with one hand at the knob for 25 seconds.

Make sure your child can handle the bat he wants before you buy it!

Before buying a bat, have your child hit with a selection of bats supplied by the league. You'll see right away which ones are too small, too big, or too heavy. With a bat that is an inch or two too long, the player might choke up a little. If he or she needs to choke up more than an inch, however, go to the next inch-size down. Before you decide to purchase a bat for your child, ask your league about any limits on bat size or weight.

SIZE MATTERS

Worth, a bat manufacturer, recently completed a research project to determine the best bat weight for players in youth baseball. The company developed a formula that divides the player's height in inches by four and adds four.

(Height ÷ 4) + 4 = Best Bat Weight

8–10 Years Old

PLAYER HEIGHT	BEST BAT WEIGHT
48 inches	16 ounces
52 inches	17 ounces
56 inches	18 ounces
60 inches	19 ounces

As kids age, Worth suggests, use weight instead of height to select the best bat weight. The formula divides the player's weight in pounds by 18 and adds 14.

(Weight ÷ 18) + 14 = Best Bat Weight

11–12 Years Old

PLAYER WEIGHT	BEST BAT WEIGHT
80 pounds	19 ounces
100 pounds	20 ounces
120 pounds	21 ounces
140 pounds	22 ounces

Gloves

A regular fielder's glove is made of leather. It has four separate fingers connected to the thumb by a leather web or pocket. A glove is a player's most important piece of equipment, so make sure the glove feels comfortable and fits your child's hand well. The player must be able to move the glove quickly to the ball. This requires a glove that's not too big and not too heavy. The player must be able to close the glove with his or her hand so that the ball does not pop out.

The glove should be in proportion to your child's hand. Balls will be harder to control with a bigger glove. Buy the smallest glove that will do the job properly for the player. The increase in glove control far outweighs the advantage of more reach.

Bring your child to a sporting goods store, and try on several different gloves. Try not to be influenced by "autographs" of famous players. When your child chooses a particular glove, test it to make sure the glove is not too loose. Place a ball in the webbing, and ask your child to hold the baseball in the glove with the palm facing downward. If the ball falls to the floor, select a smaller model.

More expensive is not always better when it comes to baseball gloves. Players just starting out will do fine with vinyl or combination vinyl and leather models. These are less expensive than leather and have pockets that bend and flex easily, giving greater glove control to small children or those with limited strength.

Remember that buying a glove is like buying a pair of shoes. The item should feel good when worn, and it will become more comfortable as it softens from use.

Hall of Fame catcher Ray Schalk displays the mitt he used in 1912 (right) next to a much larger model from 1963.

■ Catching Equipment

A catcher on the field wears a padded chest protector, plastic shin guards, a protective cup (female catchers, too!), a helmet, and a padded mask with narrow metal bars across the face. Organized leagues always supply the catcher's equipment, but parents should keep in mind that the equipment, while still safe, is not specially "fitted" for their children. Parents may consider purchasing catcher's gear for an older, high school-age child, but only if the athlete is serious about the position and wishes to specialize at it. Most experts agree that youngsters should play all the positions and keep from specializing at a particular position until at least 13 years old.

A GLOVE STORY

Nobody touches NOMAR GARCIAPARRA'S glove. Nomar won't let anyone else put a hand inside it. "I never throw my glove," says the Boston Red Sox All-Star shortstop. "I place it down in the dugout."

Why does Nomar take such special care of his equipment? When he was 6 years old, Nomar joined a tee ball league and needed a baseball glove. "My father bought me a glove for $125, which our family really couldn't afford," he recalls.

"So I made sure it would last and took care of it. I used the same glove through high school. If somebody threw my glove, I was mad. There was a respect I had for my equipment."

■ Practice Skills

This chapter outlines some basic activities you can do with your child or a group of kids to help them improve their baseball skills. The games and drills work whether you're playing with just your child in the backyard or coaching a team. Even if you don't plan to coach, the skills outlined here will help you become more knowledgeable about your child's play. Who knows? You may even amaze your child with a solid piece of advice. Keep two things in mind at all times: First, this is supposed to be fun. Second, practice makes perfect. These principles apply to parents, as well as kids.

Playing baseball requires four main areas of skill: throwing, catching, hitting, and base running. Whenever you go out to play, be creative, and make drills short and fun. For younger players, you might want to use a rubber, low-impact safety ball or tennis ball to eliminate the fear factor. Don't rush. It takes time to develop baseball skills. You don't have to be a major league star to teach good baseball techniques to your child. If you pay attention to the fundamentals outlined in this book, your child will progress quickly and avoid forming bad habits that are difficult to break.

Throwing

Whenever you practice, whether it's just a catch in the backyard or a formal team practice, set aside time at the beginning to work on good overhand throwing habits. Have a player face a target with a ball in the throwing hand. The player brings the glove-side foot forward while rotating the shoulders and hips back. Then the player pushes his or her weight back on the ball-side foot. At this point, the player's glove should be pointed toward the target, the throwing arm should be extended back, and the wrist should be cocked.

As the arm comes forward to make the throw, the player should shift the weight to the front foot. At the midpoint of the throw, the throwing arm comes forward, and the glove hand extends down to the knee. As the shoulders rotate back, make sure the player's body is square to the target as the throwing hand extends down on the follow-through.

Throwing

1. Get ready   2. Aim and shift weight   3. Release

33

Many kids shortcut the throw and use only their arms while facing squarely forward. Encourage your child to get in the habit of turning his or her body and following through. This will help the child throw more accurately and with greater force.

Throwing Drills

Just as it takes two to tango, it takes two people to have a catch. However, you can buy "pitch-back" screens that allow kids to practice throwing by themselves. Ask the local sporting goods store to recommend a good one. In addition, kids can practice their throwing accuracy with a simple target drill. Mark a target box on a backstop, fence, or garage door with tape. Then position the player about 15 feet from the target. Have the player practice accuracy by trying to hit the target from various distances while using proper throwing fundamentals.

Pitching

In leagues that allow older kids to pitch, the role of the pitcher should be to allow batters to put the ball in play. Nothing is more boring (to fans and players alike) than a game with a lot of walks. Coaches should choose pitchers who throw strikes. Don't be fooled by a beautiful pitching motion if the player can't hit the side of a barn. If your child wants to pitch, tell him or her not to be concerned with velocity or ability to get strikeouts. All that matters is control and throwing the ball over the plate within the strike zone.

Don't allow young pitchers to throw curveballs, sliders, split-fingered fastballs, or any other pitches that may strain unde-veloped arms, elbows, and shoulders. Stress the effectiveness of changing speeds to keep batters off balance. Also, players below high school level should not merely pitch, as if they were specialists. Young kids should pitch only one game per week and play other positions, too. Most youth leagues have rules governing the number of innings per game and the number of games per week that a player is allowed to pitch. Check to make sure your league observes these rules.

Catching

In baseball, players have to catch the ball when it's thrown by other players, when it's hit in the air, and when it's hit on the ground. In all three cases, proper catching technique begins with the player in the ready position. Players should stand facing home plate, with their knees slightly bent and feet square. Weight should be placed on the balls of the feet, and the glove should be at waist level. Have your young player practice this stance whenever he or she is in the field.

When a thrown ball or a fly ball comes a player's way, he or she should always try to catch the ball with two hands. The arms should be extended to reach out for the ball, but the player shouldn't stab at it. The glove should be kept wide open to accept the ball, and the other hand should be close by to help guide the ball into the glove. A player's arms should give with the ball as it enters the glove.

Catching

1. Set up

2. Keep eyes on ball as it enters glove

When a ground ball is hit to an infielder, the player must position his or her body in front of the ball. A player should always try to field a ground ball while moving toward the ball. He or she should never back up on a grounder, because then the ball will play the fielder, instead of the fielder playing the ball. A player in fielding position for a grounder should have the glove on the ground, touching the dirt, because if the ball bounces awkwardly, it's easier to go from the ground up to field the ball.

Fly Ball Drill

This is a good fly ball drill you can do in your yard or on the field. Stand about 20 feet away from a player and throw the ball high enough for him or her to run under it. Begin by throwing the ball only a few feet higher than the player's head, and progress to high fly balls.

Ground Ball Drills

A good ground ball drill emphasizes the fundamentals of footwork and positioning. Stand a few feet apart from a player and roll a baseball back and forth with him or her. Have the player work on getting the body down low, reaching out with soft hands, and letting the arms give with the ball. Players can practice fielding grounders solo by using a wall drill. Standing about 15 feet away, a child can throw a tennis ball at a wall and field the caroms and rebounds, first with bare hands and then using a glove.

Fielding a grounder

1. Move to ball   2. Look ball into glove   3. Set up to throw

Helpful Hint

If a ball is above waist level, a player should keep his or her two thumbs together with the glove pointing up to field it. If the ball is below the waist, the player should keep the two pinkies together with the glove pointing down. Young players may have a hard time with this drill and always try to catch the ball with the glove facing one direction or another. The ability to "turn the glove over" while trying to catch the ball comes with practice and maturity.

REAL-LIFE EXAMPLE

It hurts to give up a home run, but it hurts even worse when a home run bounces off your head! That's what happened to JOSÉ CANSECO during a game in 1993. José was playing right field for the Texas Rangers. Carlos Martinez of the Cleveland Indians swatted a deep fly ball. José ran to the wall, jumped, and reached for the ball with his glove.

José missed the ball, but the ball didn't miss him. It hit him on the head and bounced over the fence for a home run. "You could hit one hundred fly balls at me, and I couldn't do that again," said José.

Team Defense

Every time a ball is hit, every player on the defensive team must go into action. Each defensive player has a responsibility, whether to field the ball, accept the throw, or back up a teammate. Talk to your child about what he or she might do in different defensive situations: "You're playing second. There's a runner on first. The batter hits a ground ball to the shortstop. What do you do?" This is a great way to pass time in the car. On the field, call out situations, and see how fast your player or players can get to their proper positions.

Base Running

Players should always run hard to first base. Have them run across the bag like a sprinter hitting a finish-line tape. This ensures that the player will still be running at top speed when crossing the base, giving him or her the best chance of beating a throw from a fielder.

It's okay to overrun first base, but not second or third. A player may not be tagged out after overrunning first as long as he or she turns to the right, away from the field of play. If a player overruns second or third base, he or she may be tagged out. Sliding is the best way to avoid a tag and stop at a base without overrunning it. Young players learning to slide typically crash into the bag because they wait too long to start their slides. A player should begin to slide about 10 feet from the base. The *bent-leg slide* is most common. The right leg is extended toward the base and the left leg is bent under the right knee to form a shape like a 4. The slide should be on the buttocks, not on the side or the hip, and one hand should be kept up over the head.

Bent-leg slide

1. **Lean back and set up leg positions**

2. **Fully extend lead leg**

3. **Slide**

Helpful Hint *Instruct players to slide feet-first only. Kids think the headfirst slide makes them faster, but it actually slows them down. Most sliding injuries occur from the headfirst slide. Never slide headfirst into home plate or into first base. Some youth leagues do not allow players to slide until they reach a certain age. Check with your league for rules regarding slides.*

Hitting

The great Red Sox slugger Ted Williams once said that hitting a baseball is the most difficult skill in all of sports to master. A batter must hit a round ball with a round bat squarely. The batter has barely one second from the time the ball is pitched until it reaches the plate. Even top major league players who maintain a .300 batting average make an out 70 percent of the time. Your young player should keep this in mind. Every player strikes out. Every player hits into double plays. Every player gets better with practice.

Proper technique will almost certainly make your young player a better hitter. It all begins with the proper stance. The batter should stand comfortably with the feet shoulder-width apart. The bat should be held near the back ear, and the elbows should be held out from the body. As the pitch approaches, the batter strides a few inches with the front foot. Beginners should keep their strides short. This stride is a timing mechanism to begin the swing.

As the batter swings directly to the ball, he or she should rotate the hips and keep the body weight centered throughout the swing. It's important to have a good hip turn. As the hips turn, the back foot also turns so that all five toes face the pitcher. The batter's front foot will also turn. Try this a few times without a bat to get the feel. Then go through the motion slowly with a bat.

The adage "Keep your eye on the ball" has many purposes. It reminds batters to first see the ball, and then hit the ball. (You can't see the ball if your eyes are shut or if you're looking down at your feet.) It's also a reminder to keep the head still. Tucking the chin slightly against the front shoulder will help keep the batter's head steady. The goal is to look down the barrel of the bat as the ball makes contact. It's okay to swing hard, but the swing should stay under control. Teach kids to attack the ball with maximum bat speed. Batters should swing slightly down at the ball and not in an uppercut or "golf swing" motion.

Hitting

1. Crouch toward plate, keep eye on the ball

2. Begin to shift weight into swing, keep eye on the ball

Everyone who loves baseball loves to hit. Kids can practice their swings alone, but you can help them with hitting fundamentals using a stationary batting tee. Inexpensive batting tees are available from most sporting goods stores, toy stores, and mass merchants. Set up the tee and ball 10 feet in front of a high fence or backstop. Then let your young slugger hack away.

Helpful Hint *When a batter grips the bat, the fingers should be relaxed; the batter shouldn't squeeze the bat too tightly. The bat should be held in the fingers, not in the palms of the hands. Young players should always choke up about an inch from the bottom of the bat handle.*

3. Shift weight fully into swing, look ball into bat, and swing through level with ground

4. Follow through

43

Accentuate the Positive

 The best way to help your child have a positive baseball experience is to be a positive sports parent. Remember, kids play sports to have fun. In this case, you should take your cue from them. Keep things positive, and you'll both have a great time. The headlines about some parents' behavior at games can be frightening, but the vast majority of sports parents are on your side. They want their kids to have fun and come away with great memories. Your role as a sports parent is simple. Support your child, but behave the same way you would in other realms of life. Apply the "golden rule" to umpires, coaches, and other parents, and you'll be an exemplary role model of which your child will be proud.

What Age to Begin?

There's no rule that states at what age a child should begin playing baseball. As a parent, you are the best judge of when your child is physically and emotionally ready to play in an organized league. It's great to encourage your child to participate, but even the most diehard baseball fans should resist the temptation to pressure their children to compete if they are not ready.

Most children are introduced to organized baseball through tee ball leagues that begin as early as kindergarten. If your 5-year-old demonstrates a desire to join in, first make certain the field of play is in safe condition. Then meet the coach or coaches to ensure that they are qualified to guide your child through this new experience. Don't be afraid to ask questions. For example: Is the emphasis on winning or on having fun? Does everyone get equal playing time? How many practices are there each week? How does the coach handle discipline? The first step to positive sports parenting is to feel that your child is safe and well cared for at practice and games. If you have confidence about these things, you can concentrate on helping your child get the most from baseball.

It's up to parents to decide when their child is ready to play baseball.

TEAM CALENDAR

Have your child write out a weekly schedule of all his or her activities. Post the schedule on the fridge or family bulletin board. Even for a young child, the act of writing out weekly activities can help him or her take responsibility for resolving conflicts and making time for school projects, as well as baseball practices and games.

■ Set Limits, Set Goals

Parents should work together with their children to set limits of participation. Never promise more time than you can deliver. Being part of a team requires a time commitment from the entire family— and sometimes requires sacrifices from every family member. If a sibling's schedule conflicts with game day, which event will be forced to take a backseat? What will you do if (when) the ballet recital or club outing occurs on the same day as a game? How do school activities and commitments fit with weekly baseball practice and the game schedule? Discussing possible alternatives in advance will aid in the decision-making process and help prevent hard feelings.

Before your child joins a league, have him or her set realistic goals regarding performance. This will help guarantee success. Remember to set goals that involve improving your child's skills—not wins or losses. Help your child understand that there will be both positive and negative experiences associated with competitive sports, and let him or her know you'll be there for support no matter what.

Get Involved

As a baseball parent, your main job is to encourage and support your child's participation. Your child will appreciate your involvement and benefit from your excitement.

Families can actively support their local leagues by assisting fundraising efforts, helping with administration, and caring for the quality of the playing fields. Most youth leagues are happy to have parents volunteer even if they can only spare a small amount of time. Consider volunteering and getting involved. You will be amazed at how much this means to your child.

Help the Coach

If your relationship with your child's coach is positive and trusting, everyone will have a great experience—regardless of whether your child's team wins or loses. Start with these simple basics. You can help the coach and your child by making sure your young athlete sleeps and eats properly. Provide your child with the proper equipment needed to play safely and to compete at the best of his or her abilities. Always inform the coach if your child is ill or was recently injured. Have your child arrive at practice and games on time and prepared to play—suited up, shoes tied, glove in hand. Finally, arrive early—never late—for pickup.

It may be difficult at first, but a parent must be prepared to trust the coach and accept that the coach will gain the child's admiration and respect. When you bring your child to practice, you're turning him or her over to the coach's care. Let the coach *coach* without undue interference or meddling.

As a rule, don't interfere with the coach's methods unless the coach has clearly made a mistake. Then discuss the issue with the coach in private—never in front of the team. This might require a meeting before the next practice or a phone call in the evening. If you cannot work out a solution, you can take the issue to the league as discussed later in this book. However, if your child misbehaves, breaks team rules, is uncooperative, or is uncontrollable, you may be required to discipline the child in cooperation with the coach. Parents generally should not threaten to keep their children from playing as a way to change their on-the-field behavior. Instead of shaping up, most kids will grow disinterested in baseball. Try to work out a plan with the coach and your child to help correct the problem. It is very important to give your child the message that the coach is in charge on the field and that you will support his or her decisions.

STAY-AT-HOME VACATIONS

If your older child makes a total commitment to baseball, the family must be prepared to support that choice. Older kids often have tournaments or playoffs that extend into vacation times. If games are scheduled during vacation, don't plan a family getaway. Instead, enjoy time off at home, and watch your child compete on the ball field. This experience can create lasting family memories.

Communicating with the Coach

Coaches are often powerful role models for children. It's your obligation as a parent to talk to the coach to see that your child will thrive under his or her tutelage.

Parents and coaches usually enjoy a common bond, because they share an interest in the child's growth as a person and as a player. Talk to the coach periodically about your child's playing ability, progress, and relations with teammates.

It is important that parents never criticize coaches in front of their children or the team. However, parents do have every right to talk privately with the coach if their child is unhappy. Even if you don't agree with the coach, talking together can help clear the air and help you explain things to your child.

Try to be as objective as possible when discussing issues with the coach. Put yourself in his or her shoes. Remember that the coach has the whole team, as well as all the parents, to consider. Always remain calm and civil when discussing issues with your child's coach. Most coaches will listen if you present your issues calmly. However, if the coach becomes angry or is unreceptive to your issues, or if you simply cannot reach a fair conclusion, take the matter to the league president. The league president's responsibility is to resolve problems between parents and coaches. If no other solution can be found, the league president may step in and place your child on another team.

■ Attending Games

By attending games and watching a few practices, you will see what your child is learning, check on his or her development during the season, and notice how the coach handles the team. However, attending every practice may not be a good idea. Ask your child if he or she wants you to come and watch. Even if your child says yes, your presence may be unnerving. If this is the case, you may have to stop going to games until your young athlete gains more confidence on the playing field.

As a schoolboy legend at Moeller High in Cincinnati, Ohio, Ken Griffey, Jr., had no problem performing in front of big league scouts. But when his dad, Reds outfielder Ken Griffey, Sr., would come to watch his son play, Junior felt pressure. He tried so hard to impress his father that he could barely hit the ball. "He didn't get a hit in front of me for six years!" says Ken, Sr.

■ Game Day

Arriving at the game on time means getting there early. Plan to arrive about half an hour early (or perhaps even earlier if you are driving a long distance) to allow your child time to gather his or her thoughts, take in the surroundings, and just relax. Half an hour also gives the

This young fan makes a play on a foul ball from the stands.

coach an opportunity to talk to parents, and it gives the players time to conduct a pregame workout.

Once you arrive, don't be surprised if your child rushes to join his or her teammates and ignores you completely. Be confident that your young player is happy you are there. The kid's focus is naturally on the team, the coach, and playing the game.

After the game, whether the team wins or loses, tell your child how much you enjoyed watching. Comment on how his or her skills are improving and how great the team played together. Avoid "coaching" comments or making suggestions about how to improve next time. It's important to let your child know you are proud no matter what the outcome is.

One parent suggested that there are only three things to say to your child after a game: "I had a great time watching you play," "You're getting so much better every game," and "What do you want to eat?"

Support from the Bleachers

When watching your child's team, always maintain your self-control, and constantly be aware of your behavior. It's fine to root loudly, but also demonstrate a sense of humor and a relaxed attitude toward the business of winning and losing. Feel free to acknowledge and even cheer good plays by the other team.

"As a parent, it's incumbent on you to ensure that [the game] is conducted in an intelligent, mature manner," says Rick Wolff, a noted sports psychologist. "Somebody has to act like an adult, so it might as well be you."

Keep your emotions under control and your personal agenda in check. Above all, don't embarrass your child or yourself. Make every comment a positive, affirming statement and you'll do just fine.

Remember: It's great to root loudly, but always keep your self-control.

■ Bleacher Creatures

No matter what happens, never criticize the coach during the game. The players won't know whom to listen to—the coach or the parents—and may become rattled and distracted.

Negative remarks from the bleachers directed at an umpire usually do nothing more than make young players unhappy. Even if the umpire is doing a poor job, it's in the best interest of your child's team for you to keep your opinions to yourself. An official's controversial call can be acknowl-edged by the spectators, but don't get personally upset about missed calls.

Umpires are human, just like players. Players make mistakes, and so do umps. Explain to your child that the umpire is in charge of the game and that you can't change that fact. No matter how bad the umpire is, each team should still keep playing their best. Parents should never confront the ump during or after the game. If you think an ump is missing calls, talk to the coach the next day and ask him or her to speak to the proper league authorities.

Winning and Losing

Parents are often unprepared for the powerful emotions they experience when watching their children compete. Dealing with losing can be an especially awkward experience for both parents and children. With a little assistance, you can help your child prepare in advance for the inevitable losses that come with any baseball season.

Allow your child to take competition seriously, and encourage commitment and dedication. But be aware that sometimes children can care too much. They can equate their self-worth with winning and losing. Should you detect this sentiment, help your child put things in proper per-spective. Having a set of personal goals on which to fall back is a big plus when a tough loss inevitably occurs.

When kids of any age experience a tough loss, they don't want to be told, "Cheer up, don't worry about it." At that moment, permit your child to feel the normal unhappiness that goes with defeat. Learn to accept your child's disappointment, as difficult as that may be. Avoid comments that your child may feel lack sincerity or that may be heard as sarcasm. Sympathize with your child's feelings, but help him or her remember that losing is a part of the game.

Children sometimes learn more from losing than they do from winning. According to Dr. George Selleck, cofounder of the Positive Sports Parenting Program, the best thing to do after a loss is to think about it and learn from it. Have your child ask these questions: Did I give it my best effort? Was I prepared both mentally and physically? Did I concentrate throughout the game? How could I have helped prevent the loss? What did the winning team do well? What could I do differently next game? Refer back to the player's personal goals. Ask how he or she did relative to those goals.

Explore the answers to these questions with your child. This will help you instill in the youngster the ideal that no matter what the final outcome, having fun and

*Chris Cardone, center, gets mobbed after hitting
a two-run home run in the sixth inning of the
1998 Little League World Series.*

doing your best are more important than
winning. These questions should also be
asked after a win. Always dole out heap-
ing portions of praise for your child's effort,
and minimize winning and losing. Most
importantly, help your child become both
a kind winner and a gracious loser.

Sometimes kids need a cooling-off
period after a tough loss. Allow them
space if necessary. Don't offer criticism—
even constructive criticism—during this
time. If your child wants more instruction
to improve playing skills, wait for him or
her to come to you.

■ You the Coach!

One way to be sure that your child's experience in youth league baseball is pleasant is to take an active role, as either head or assistant coach. Volunteering in some capacity is your obligation as a parent. If you already play the game, you'll be in demand as a coach. If you never played but want to learn, your child's coach may need an assistant. And this year's assistant is often next year's coach.

Coaches should have two aims: to teach the game and to make practice and games fun. It's easy to have fun playing baseball, but it takes an imaginative coach to have fun at practice. The American Sport Education Program (ASEP) encourages all coaching parents to stress the "fun and fundamentals" of playing organized youth baseball.

"The ol' hat trick"

"Youth coaches have the power to turn children off to sports forever, or to make sports a lifelong passion," says Fred Engh, founder of the National Alliance for Youth Sports and the author of *Why Johnny Hates Sports*. "With the proper training, knowledge, and skills, a coach can improve [children's lives] immensely, and help prepare them for the future."

Coaching Your Kid

Many famous athletes have enjoyed successful careers while being coached by a parent. Golf's Tiger Woods, tennis's Venus and Serena Williams, and baseball's Cal Ripken, Jr., to name a few, have all been coached by their parents—with whom they still maintain healthy, positive relationships.

Still, you should never assume that your child wants you to coach the team. Explain why you wish to be involved, and ask your child if he or she wants you to coach. If the answer is yes, explain what your new responsibilities are and how they may affect your parent-child relationship during practices and games.

Once you step on the playing field and begin coaching your child, it is very important not to confuse the two roles of parent and coach. If you do, it will send mixed signals that will confuse your youngster and the other team members. Avoiding

59

the urge to be a parent during games and practice sessions will help keep your role as coach clear in your child's mind. Off the field, simply follow the guidelines for positive sports parenting.

Parenting itself is a tough enough job. Being a parent and coaching your own child only makes the task more difficult. For the child, there may be a heavy burden of expectation because Mom or Dad is coaching the team. For the parent you may find yourself being harder on your child than on his or her teammates. This may be because you don't want to show favoritism, or you want to convince other parents that your child doesn't receive preferential treatment.

If you steer clear of these traps, the time you spend coaching your child will produce a lasting bond between the two of you. Coaching can provide a rare opportunity for both parent and child to work together toward a common goal.

"The obvious advantages to coaching your child," says sports psychologist Mary Casper, "[are] spending more time with your child, sharing in their successes, and coaching a sport you love."

LIKE FATHER, LIKE SON

The list of major league players who have been managed by their fathers includes the following:

Ken Griffey, Sr. & Jr.

Son	Father	Team
Dale Berra	Yogi	New York Yankees
Brian McRae	Hal	Kansas City Royals
Cal Ripken, Jr.	Cal, Sr.	Baltimore Orioles
Moises Alou	Felipe	Montreal Expos
Ken Griffey, Jr.	Ken, Sr.	Cincinnati Reds

■ How Players Learn

Learning to play baseball is no different from learning any other skill. The first requirement is personal desire. If a player is excited about baseball, he or she will want to learn much more than the child who remains detached. If you supply your players with lots of positive feedback and approval, you will have a team of eager learners.

Kids learn in three basic ways: Others instruct them; somebody acts as an example for them; and they discover for themselves. Kids do best when they employ all three methods, and coaches teach best when applying them in the proper order.

First, make sure you know the names of all of the kids on your team! Introduce a skill so that young players know what they are about to learn and why. Always explain the importance of the skill. Then demonstrate the skill, because young learners need pictures as examples, not just words. If you or one of your assistants is unable to perform the skill correctly, have an experienced player demonstrate.

The most important thing about practice is that it should be fun!

Teach the separate parts of the skill—break it down, and have the players perform each part correctly. Emphasize the basics so that youngsters have a solid foundation on which to build. Then look for continuous improvement from all players. This will help your team develop confidence knowing there's no pressure to be perfect.

■ How Successful Coaches Communicate

Errors are a major factor of every youth baseball game, and your players will make their share of mistakes during practice, too. Don't be too quick to criticize. Even great fielders make their share of mistakes. One of the best, outfielder Willie Davis of the Los Angeles Dodgers, made three errors in one inning of Game 2 of the 1966 World Series. So reiterate the details of a drill, and continue to instill an overall positive attitude. Younger kids particularly need reassurance because they often doubt their abilities.

Your players will look to you for constant feedback. Whatever the message you're trying to convey, the manner in which you say it is at least as important as what you say. Keep your

Game 2

Thursday, October 6, At Los Angeles

Baltimore	AB.	R.	H.	RBI.	PO.	A.
Aparicio, ss	5	0	2	1	4	1
Blefary, lf	5	0	0	0	1	0
F. Robinson, rf	3	2	1	0	1	0
B. Robinson, 3b	4	1	1	0	1	1
Powell, 1b	3	1	2	1	8	0
D. Johnson, 2b	4	0	2	1	2	4
Blair, cf	3	1	0	0	4	0
Etchebarren, c	3	1	0	0	6	0
Palmer, p	4	0	0	0	0	2
Totals	34	6	8	3	27	8
Los Angeles	AB.	R.	H.	RBI.	PO.	A.
Wills, ss	4	0	0	0	3	1
Gilliam, 3b	4	0	0	0	2	3
W. Davis, cf	4	0	0	0	2	0
Fairly, rf	3	0	0	0	3	0
Lefebvre, 2b	3	0	0	0	3	0
L. Johnson, lf	4	0	1	0	1	0
Roseboro, c	4	0	1	0	8	1
Parker, 1b	2	0	1	0	5	1
Koufax, p	2	0	0	0	0	1
Perranoski, p	0	0	0	0	0	1
Regan, p	0	0	0	0	0	0
aT. Davis	1	0	1	0	0	0
Brewer, p	0	0	0	0	0	0
Totals	31	0	4	0	27	8

Baltimore					0 0 0	0 3 1	0 2 0—6
Los Angeles					0 0 0	0 0 0	0 0 0—0

Baltimore	IP.	H.	R.	ER.	BB.	SO.
Palmer (W)	9	4	0	0	3	6

Los Angeles	IP.	H.	R.	ER.	BB.	SO.
Koufax (L)	6	6	4	1	2	2
Perranoski	1⅓	2	2	2	1	1
Regan	⅔	0	0	0	0	0
Brewer	1	0	0	0	0	1

aSingled for Regan in eighth. E—Gilliam, W. Davis 3, Fairly, Perranoski. DP—Los Angeles 1. LOB—Baltimore 6. Los Angeles 7. 2B—L. Johnson, Aparicio. 3B—F. Robinson. SH—Powell. WP—Regan, Palmer. U—Chylak (A.L.), Pelekoudas (N.L.), Rice (A.L.), Steiner (N.L.), Drummond (A.L.) and Jackowski (N.L.). T—2:26. A—55,947.

Willie Davis, a great fielder, committed three errors in one inning during the second game of the 1966 World Series voice calm. A smile can say as much as a thousand words. When talking to a youngster one-on-one, kneel down to his or her eye level. You'll be amazed at how much this simple gesture helps kids listen.

Baseball can sometimes seem over-whelming to kids because there are so many difficult skills to master. When you are working with a frustrated player, remember that nothing turns off a young-ster faster than negative feedback. Try to begin every conversation with a positive statement. You can always compliment the player's hustle or enthusiasm even if he or she needs work on a particular skill. Make your criticisms specific and constructive, and your players will respond. Be sure to compliment the player when you see improvement in a skill that you've previously criticized.

Keep the players focused on what to do rather than what not to do. Instead of saying, "Don't throw that way," you might say, "Grip the ball this way." Use words that reward the effort, not the outcome. When a player boots a grounder, don't focus on the physical error. Concentrate instead on correcting the reason for the error—"Keep your glove down"—and don't try to squeeze in too much information.

If there's one simple rule to being a successful communicator, it's to be an active listener. When coaching young kids, much of your time is spent answering questions about baseball. Listen carefully, and you'll know when your players are ready to excel at the next level.

■ The Practice

Every good coach arrives prepared. Have a specific plan when you come to practice that lists what you will be working on that day. Draw diagrams to illustrate fielding, base running, and batting drills. Figure out a time schedule for each drill the night before, and chart it on paper. Be flexible. Have a few alternate options ready in case some kids don't show.

What you plan to accomplish during a given practice session must be reasonable for the maturity level of your players. Since younger children are easily distracted and have shorter attention spans, a long demonstration or explanation will bore them. Divide the team into small groups, and spend no more than 10 minutes on the introduction, demonstration, and explanation phase of the skill you wish to teach.

Make use of your assistant coaches (if available) by having them direct drills, each covering one aspect of hitting, pitching, running, or fielding. Concentrate on teaching the basics, and move on to more complex activities only after the players have mastered the simpler techniques. Don't get too technical about a skill. Just set up a simple challenge to foster the child's own internal motivation.

SAMPLE PRACTICE DAY CHECKLIST

- ❏ Arrive early to set up equipment so the practice can begin on time.
- ❏ Discuss what you want to accomplish that day.
- ❏ Do some stretching exercises and warm-up throwing as a team.
- ❏ Go through stations: hitting, pitching, defense.
- ❏ Run bases.
- ❏ Run a scrimmage or situation drills.
- ❏ Meet for announcements.
- ❏ Clean up.

■ Keep the Flow

An easy way to make practice fun is a team activity, such as a scrimmage. Simply roll out the balls, and choose up sides.

Better yet, create situational drills by assigning each player to a defensive position and appointing other players as base runners. Call out the scenario: "No outs, bases loaded." Then you, as coach, hit (or throw) the ball, causing your team to react. This enables the players to begin to grasp the game's intricate strategies and feel the quickened pulse of baseball's unique rhythms.

Sometimes it's appropriate to interrupt a scrimmage to instruct a player. Yet if you cut in too often, the team won't enjoy a fluid practice. As a general rule, it's better to allow play to continue than to stop a scrimmage, even for moderate fine-tuning. Whenever you single out a player, you risk making that child feel as if he or she has been put on the spot.

Helpful Hint *In addition to teaching athletic skills, baseball practices should develop a player's endurance, promote strength, and increase flexibility. But sit-ups or extra laps should never be given as punishment. This sends the wrong message about exercise. Having unruly players sit on the bench for a couple of minutes is usually a better solution. Most kids want to be in the game and will respond quickly to being sidelined.*

Game Time

When the players arrive, they'll have the usual pregame jitters. As coach, you should have a pregame routine to keep the players busy as the big moment approaches—just stick with easy throwing and jogging. Avoid last-minute skills instruction. Game day is not the time to introduce new skills.

Fifteen minutes before the game, gather everyone together, read the batting order and fielding assignments, offer brief advice, and tell the substitutes what their roles will be and when to get ready. Get the players excited, and remind them that their individual performance and achievement is more important than winning or losing.

■ Be a Motivator

During the game, the coach's voice should be heard cheering for everybody. It can occasionally be heard yelling the name of a daydreaming player picking flowers in the outfield. Otherwise, limit your well-meaning advice to practices, and freely give out positive feedback throughout the game. As a coach, one of the worst things you can do to a player is to give instruction during the game. It's counterproductive to give a player hitting instruction while he or she is on deck—or worse yet, to give directions between each pitch.

As coach, don't call all the shots. Allow the players to conduct their own game as much as possible, assume leadership roles, and share the decision-making process with you. Make substitutions often, but don't "over-manage" the game. Let the kids play. You'll all have more fun—win or lose.

■ Turn Down the Volume

Quality coaching starts with enthusiastic involvement—but enthusiasm is different from an ambitious desire to win. Ambitious coaches push their players too hard, and most kids react negatively to this type of pressure. Try to understand a child's unique and often fragile makeup, and be sensitive to your players' emotions.

Above all, don't seek personal recognition at the expense of the team. Your behavior should demonstrate respect for the game, and that will help the team develop a sense of honor. A heavy-handed coach comes across as trying to prove him- or herself through the players. This almost always backfires—the team does not respond and the kids lose interest.

■ Communicating with Parents

Prior to the first practice, it's important that the coach call a mandatory meeting with the parents and players. Say what you expect from the kids and from the parents. Outline your goals, emphasizing the league philosophy. Reinforce the league rules and mandates. Stress the importance of getting to practice on time, calling if you can't attend a team function, and informing the coaches about any medical problems, such as asthma. Explain to the group that while we all want to win, the first rule is to have fun.

Distribute a roster with names and phone numbers of everybody on the team. Let parents know their children's game and practice schedules in advance so that families can arrange their calendars and coordinate carpools.

Assure parents that you are knowledgeable about baseball (you've read this book, after all) and care about their children's well-being. Get to know the parents at the beginning of the season so that your initial meeting is under neutral circumstances. You don't want your first contact with a parent to be a complaint about a child's playing time.

Open communication with parents by getting them involved in a discreet way before and after games. Assign parents the duties of setting up and putting away equipment or helping with pregame field preparations. Take advantage of your time together by starting up a conversation with parents. Let them know you wish to hear their comments face-to-face. Then be receptive to whatever they have to say.

Helpful Hint *At the end of practices, call your team together for brief announcements. Discuss the time and place of the next practice, and distribute any printed information you want to be taken home. Always remind parents of pickup times, and encourage them to be prompt. You are their children's coach, not a baby-sitter.*

■ Kiss the Ump

It's imperative that coaches treat umpires with respect and understanding before, during, and after games. Don't refer to an umpire as "Blue" or "Mr. Ump." Before the game, greet the umpires by name (or introduce yourself), and make casual conversation about the upcoming contest. Umpires are trying to do their jobs just as hard as you are. And since an umpire doesn't tell you how to coach, don't tell the umpire how to do his or her job.

Like coaches and players, umpires are human and will make mistakes. Direct your players never to argue with an umpire. Only the coach should challenge an umpire and only on very rare occasions. Never dispute balls and strikes or a close call. Should you, as coach, disagree with an umpire's interpretation of the rulebook (and you are positive that you know the rules), state your case simply and directly. Don't get in the ump's face. Make your point in a controlled voice, and then prepare to listen to the umpire's point of view. Finally, remember that the umpire has the last word.

The way you treat umpires will influence the way your players behave. If you respect umpires as the game's final authorities and do not treat them as enemies, you will set a good example for your players. The more you communicate with umpires in a positive, respectful manner, the better they will work with you and your team.

■ Be Safe, Not Sorry

 Few things are more frightening for parents than the thought of their child suffering a sports-related injury. You will be relieved to learn that severe injuries to youth baseball players are rare. Most often, players get scrapes, bruises, and—to a lesser extent—minor sprains and strains. Baseball injuries are less frequent and less serious than skateboarding or rollerblading injuries.

Many injuries can easily be avoided if a responsible adult spends time to ensure that the field of play and the equipment used by the children are free of hazards. Coaches and parents should report dangerous field conditions and request any necessary maintenance, suspending play until safe conditions have been restored. Damaged or unsafe equipment must be replaced immediately.

Your local baseball organization should require all players to undergo a routine physical exam and to present a physician's consent form before being allowed to play. The coach must know if a player is asthmatic or diabetic or suffers from any other chronic ailment. Coaches should always bring kids' medical paperwork to each game and practice for easy reference in case of injury or accident.

REAL-LIFE EXAMPLES

BOB GIBSON of the St. Louis Cardinals suffered from asthma when he was a kid but learned to control it and grew up to be a Hall of Fame pitcher. Gibson won seven consecutive World Series games and set a series record with 17 strikeouts in a game.

■ Coaching Safety

Responsible coaches can juggle safety, teaching, and fun. This is accomplished by planning activities in such a way that the progression between drills keeps risk at a minimum. When executing practice drills, players should be matched with one another according to physical maturity to create the safest possible environment.

All sports have inherent risks. Injury-free participation requires proper supervision. Coaches must never assume that young athletes know how to wear protective equipment. It's up to the coach to explain to the players why the protective gear is used and how to use it properly. And it's up to parents to make sure they are familiar with protective equipment and how it is used.

Young kids may not intuitively know how dangerous it can be to swing a bat near unsuspecting teammates or understand why wearing a helmet is mandatory even for base runners. Reduce the risk of injury by instructing and warning players about the hazards of playing organized ball. Above all, never make exceptions to safety rules.

■ Minor Injuries

It's the coach's duty to provide a first-aid kit and ice packs for bumps and bruises. The coach is most often the one in charge if and when an injury occurs. Therefore, it's the coach's responsibility to be informed about basic emergency care. All coaches should become familiar with procedures for treating minor injuries. In addition, the Red Cross conducts first-aid classes that can help both coaches and parents feel more confident in case an accident occurs. Parents should be familiar with the league's emergency procedures and policies about treating injuries.

■ Major Injuries

The severity and nature of an injury will determine how actively involved a coach should be in treating the injury. When injured body parts become swollen and discolored, ASEP recommends caring for the injury by following the PRICE method. PRICE is an acronym to help you remember the steps to take toward initial treatment.

P—Protect the child from further trauma.

R—Rest the injured area to promote healing.

I—Ice the area to reduce pain and swelling.

C—Compress the wound by wrapping an ice pack on the area.

E—Elevate the injury to prevent blood from pooling.

■ Coach—Don't Be a Hero

When a young player is seriously injured, the coach's first concern is naturally the child's well-being. But head, neck, and back injuries, broken bones, or loss of consciousness after a collision are not the types of injuries that a volunteer coach should attempt to treat. Still, an educated coach will know what steps to take for basic emergency care. Here are some guidelines for coaches to follow:

• Have a written record of telephone numbers for nearby emergency care facilities, and carry that record with you at all times.

• Calm an injured athlete, and keep people away. Instruct players on the field to "take a knee" and others to remain seated on the bench.

• Never move an injured athlete.

• Assign an assistant coach or appointed adult the responsibility of locating the nearest phone or using a cellular phone to contact emergency medical help.

• Stay with the child until medical personnel arrive at the scene.

• If another player is involved in a situation that causes an injury, be sure an assistant coach talks to the child to relieve any guilt feelings associated with the injury.

• Check with league officials regarding CPR training and legal issues for which you may be held liable. The coaching experience should be safe for you, as well as your players.

■ Shaping Up

Even limber, young players must prepare their bodies for vigorous activity. A 10-minute period of easy warm-up and stretching is sufficient for youngsters' muscles, tendons, and ligaments to withstand the exertion of playing baseball. This warm-up will help prevent injury.

Before practice, players should stretch four main areas: upper body, shoulders, groin, and legs. Coaches should be certain that players loosen up their throwing arms before performing skills or drills that require them to throw the ball. When coaching warm-ups, keep players far enough apart so that they don't intrude into each other's personal space. Even a catch in the backyard should begin with a period of warm-up throws and simple stretches.

At the other end, each practice should finish with a 10-minute period of light exercise. This will cool down the athletes' body temperature and allow the pulse rate to return to the resting state.

Good coaches make conditioning drills fun. Besides a routine of calisthenics and stretching, include a skill component such as base running in your conditioning program to prevent players from getting bored.

Sean Farrell practices before the championship game of the 2000 Little League World Series.

• *Players should never stretch to the point of pain.*

- *Each stretch should be held for at least 10 seconds.*
- *Both sides of the body should be stretched equally.*
- *Players should not hold their breaths during a stretch.*

◼ Water Breaks

Physical activity in hot, humid weather will take a toll on a player's body. Make sure you always have a large supply of cool water available for players to drink.

Coaches must provide water breaks for players before, during, and after practice. Parents can help by bringing coolers of ice water to practices or games on hot days. Help the coach by volunteering to be the Water Mom or Dad at the next practice. Make sure your athlete has at least one or two water bottles at all practices and games.

Make sure your player knows never to wait until he or she feels thirsty before drinking fluids. In most cases, dehydration occurs even before players feel thirsty, so remind your child to take plenty of water breaks, especially on hot days.

■ Nutrition Counts

Explain to your child that his or her body is an engine, and like any engine, it needs fuel to operate. Junk food is junk fuel, which causes the engine to sputter. In contrast, high-performance fuel comes from a diet high in complex carbohydrates and low in fat.

Young athletes need to supply their bodies with extra energy to keep up with the demands of practices and games. Let your child know the importance of healthy eating and the dangers that can come from efforts to lose weight too quickly. Active kids need lots of calories (about 2,000 a day for 7- to 10-year-olds) to meet their bodies' growth and energy demands.

If your child sometimes gets weary late in games, a candy bar may provide quick energy. Parents sometimes fear a sugar rush will be followed by a sugar crash. But unless your child is extremely sensitive to sugar or hasn't eaten anything for a long time, one candy bar eaten during a game will not affect performance one way or another. Kids do need to eat often, so if it has been a while since lunch, a snack might help.

This coed team from Santa Cruz Valley, Arizona, discusses strategy between innings during the second round of the Little League Softball World Series in August 2000.

■ Coed Teams

It's important that coaches of coed teams treat boys and girls equally. They should make as few distinctions as possible between the sexes and should not make special exceptions for either gender. Young boys and girls are physically similar in many ways. In fact, during elementary school years, girls often mature faster physically than boys. It's not uncommon at younger levels for girls to dominate play on coed teams.

Coaches should not set up competitions between the boys and girls on the team. Instead, foster team spirit and cooperation among all the players. Boys and girls are equally aggressive and competitive when it comes to learning sports, and both are equally eager to win. Offer them both the same measure of encouragement, praise, and support.

■ Special-Needs Athletes

Your local league should be able to provide you with information about special-needs athletes. You can also contact such organizations as Disabled Sports USA and Special Olympics International for more details.

Parents of able-bodied children can help their kids understand that special-needs children want to participate alongside their friends. Both parents and coaches should give these young athletes the same support and encouragement they offer their able-bodied counterparts. Organized sports leagues must make reasonable accommodations to include children with disabilities, and coaches must make certain all athletes are accepted by their teammates. Often, the persistence and optimism displayed by a special-needs athlete can motivate other kids to strive higher. The qualities of these athletes can instill in all kids a sense of tolerance and patience with individuals different from them.

REAL-LIFE EXAMPLE

JIM ABBOTT was born without a right hand but still became a successful major league pitcher. In 1993, Jim pitched a no-hitter for the New York Yankees.

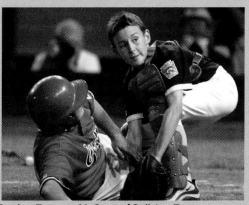

Catcher Terrence McConn of Bellaire, Texas, tags out Michael Schwartz of Davenport, Iowa, during the 2000 Little League World Series.

Life Lessons

Playing baseball will help your child stay active and enthusiastic about sports. In addition, kids who play sports at an early age are likely to be healthier individuals and have a lifetime love of sports.

Youth baseball is often a child's first introduction to his or her own competitive nature. Before playing baseball, your child was probably content with play that consisted of fantasy, spontaneity, and creativity. So why mess with a good thing? It's healthy for children to develop commitments to the activities they enjoy, to take pride in how they perform, and to dedicate themselves to achieve important goals. Commitment, pride, and dedication are very useful life skills.

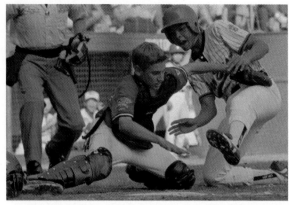

Chia-Chen Yang of Taipei, Taiwan, is safe at home as catcher Craig Stinson of Cranston, Rhode Island, drops the ball in the 1996 Little League World Series.

■ Go Team!

Kids playing youth baseball are just beginning to form attitudes that will affect them for the rest of their lives. These will include healthy competition through fair play, the cooperation and camaraderie associated with teamwork, and the benefits of physical exercise.

The ages of 5 to 12 are when a child's awareness about sportsmanship is put to the test. Learning how to congratulate the winners or console the losers is critical for a child's moral growth and ethical maturity. Sportsmanship out in the real world—call it social compromise and cooperation—is an important value for parents to impart to their children.

In this sense, sports also help develop character. Individuals with strong character are people who tend to have control over their emotions. Young athletes in organized leagues will soon understand that when they behave poorly on the field, their actions reflect negatively on the entire team.

REAL-LIFE EXAMPLE

ERNIE BANKS of the Chicago Cubs always played with a smile on his face. The Hall of Famer never appeared in the World Series, but "Mr. Cub" still loved the game, despite always playing on losing teams. Banks often said, "The only way to find out if you're a good sport is by losing."

■ Accentuate the Positive

For parents, always guide your child to strive for realistic goals. For coaches, pay attention to each child's ability level, and motivate that child to experience the simple joy of mastering new skills. When both parents and coaches remember the mantra, "Reward effort, not result," the youth baseball experience will be a positive one for all our kids.

■ Books

Wolff, Rick. *Coaching Kids for Dummies.* IDG Books Worldwide, 2000.

Wolff, Rick. *Good Sports: A Concerned Parent's Guide to Little League and Other Competitive Youth Sports.* Dell, 1993.

Wolff, Rick. *Playing Better Baseball.* Human Kinetics Publishers, 1997.

American Sport Education Program. *Coaching Youth Baseball.* Human Kinetics Publishers, 1996.

Feldman, Jay. *Hitting.* Little Simon, 1991.

Kindall, Jerry and John Winkin, eds. *The Baseball Coaching Bible.* Human Kinetics Publishers, 2000.

Kreutzer, Peter and Ted Kerley. *Little League's Official How-to-Play Baseball Book.* Doubleday, 1990.

McIntosh, Ned. *Managing Little League Baseball.* Contemporary Books, 2000.

Zinsser, Nate. *Dear Dr. Psych: A Kids' Guide to Handling Sports Problems.* Little, Brown & Company, 1991.

■ Videos

The 59-Minute Baseball Practice. Thomas Craven Film Corporation. Youth Sports Club, 1999.

■ Publications

Baseball Parent
4437 Kingstone Pike #2204
Knoxville, TN 37919-5226
(423) 523-1274
http://www.baseball-parent.com
Newsletter-style magazine (8 to 20 pages) published six times a year for the parents and coaches of youth baseball players.

Baseball America 2001 Directory
PO Box 2089
Durham, NC 27702
(919) 682-9635
www.baseballamerica.com
 The 18th annual edition is a complete guide
 of addresses and phone numbers for major
 league organizations, as well as the minors,
 independents, and youth baseball leagues.

■ National Youth Baseball Organizations

All American Amateur Baseball Association
331 Parkway Drive
Zanesville, OH 43701
(740) 453-8531
http://www.otterbein.edu/home/fac/RGRJTRMN/
 aaaba.html

Amateur Athletic Union
PO Box 10000
Lake Buena Vista, FL 32803
(407) 934-7200
http://www.aausports.org/cgiin/mytp/home/
 index.jsp

American Legion Baseball
PO Box 1055
Indianapolis, IN 46206
(317) 630-1213
http://www.legion.org

Babe Ruth Baseball
1770 Brunswick Pike
PO Box 5000
Trenton, NJ 08638
(609) 695-1434
http://www.baberuthleague.org

Dixie Youth Baseball and Softball
PO Box 231536
Montgomery, AL 36123
(334) 242-8395
http://www.dixie.org

Little League Baseball
PO Box 3485
Williamsport, PA 17701
(570) 326-1921
http://www.littleleague.org

National Amateur Baseball Federation
PO Box 705
Bowie, MD 20715
(301) 262-5005
http://www.nabf.com

National Association of Police Athletic Leagues
618 U.S. Highway 1, Suite 201
North Palm Beach, FL 33408
(561) 844-1823
http://www.nationalpal.org

Pony Baseball
PO Box 225
Washington, PA 15301
(724) 225-1060
http://www.pony.org

Reviving Baseball in Inner Cities
245 Park Avenue
New York, NY 10167
(212) 931-7897
http://www.mlb.com/u/baseball/mlbcom/
    headquarters/develop_revivingbaseball2000.html

T-Ball USA Association
2499 Main Street
Stratford, CT 06615
(203) 381-1449
http://www.teeballusa.org

U.S. Amateur Baseball Association
7101 Lake Ballinger Way
Edmonds, WA 98026
(425) 776-7130
http://www.usaba.com

■ Other Organizations

Disabled Sports USA
451 Hungerford Drive
Suite 100
Rockville, MD 20850
(301) 217-0960
http://www.dsusa.org

Positive Sports Parenting Program
Dr. George Selleck, cofounder
PO Box 1429
Sugar Land, TX 77479
(281) 565-2234
drselleck@earthlink.net

Websites

http://www.athingortwo.com
This is the Website for *A Thing or Two Media*.
Find out more on *A Thing or Two about Sports*
books. You'll also find the latest set of helpful
Web links for youth sports.

http://www.sportsparenting.org
This is the Website for the Center for Sports
Parenting, a national clearinghouse for parents
who have any and all questions about kids
playing sports.

http://www.nays.org
The National Alliance for Youth Sports provides
a one-stop site for parents and coaches in
youth sports. You can find information on being
a good coach, setting up parent programs, and
the organization's education programs.

http://www.juniorbaseball.com
This Website for "America's Youth Baseball
Magazine" covers all the bases in its Skills
Clinic. It even has great advice on how to
break in a glove.

http://www.nays.org
This is the site for the National Alliance for
Youth Sports, a leading advocate for safe,
positive, and fun sports.

http://www.positivecoach.org
This Website is for the Positive Coaching
Alliance. The Resources page provides a link
to Positive Coaching Scripts: If you are a coach
who wants to introduce a Positive Coaching
theme to your players, try using one of the scripts.
The site also has a Positive Coach's bookshelf.

http://www.thejugscompany.com
This is a one-stop shopping site for safety
equipment—plus there is a coaching corner.

CHAPTER 9

Q: At what age should my child begin playing in a league?

A: There's no rule that states at what age a child should begin playing baseball. As a parent, you're the best judge of when your child is physically and emotionally ready to play in an organized league. It's okay to encourage participation, but even the most diehard baseball fans shouldn't pressure their children to compete.

Q: My child is stocky and has a coach who wants him to lose weight. Is it safe to put a child on a low-calorie diet?

A: Coaches should never tell young athletes to lose weight for a sport. Active kids need lots of calories (about 2,000 a day for 7- to 10-year-olds) to meet their growth and energy demands. According to the experts at the International Center for Sports Nutrition, children should not be put on weight-loss programs. Of course, you should teach your child to eat a healthy, balanced diet, and if a child is truly obese, consult a doctor.

Q: My daughter becomes depressed whenever her team loses. Should I try and cheer her up?

A: If your child stays down after a loss, ignoring her other responsibilities, it's your job to help her put things in proper perspective. After a disappointing outcome, a child should be permitted a reasonable time to be unhappy. Don't be surprised if you become a temporary target for her anger and frustration. Depending on her personality, it may be a good idea to allow her a cooling-off period after a particularly tough loss. But remind her that losing is part of the game as much as winning. Focus on her personal goals and try to find positive things she can take from the experience.

Q: If I coach my own child, how should I treat my child on the field?

A: It is very important not to confuse the two roles of parent and coach. If you do, it will confuse your youngster and the team. Avoid the urge to be a parent during games and practice sessions. Off the field, reaffirm your love for your child and practice positive sports parenting as outlined in this book.

Q: I coach a coed team. Should I have different expectations for boys and girls?

A: Coaches of coed teams should treat boys and girls equally. Make as few distinctions as possible between the sexes. Young boys and girls are physically similar in many ways. In fact, during elementary school years, girls often mature faster physically than boys, so it's not uncommon at younger levels for girls to dominate play on coed teams.

Q: Are sports drinks better than water for kid athletes?

A: Sports drinks are good for marathoners, triathletes, and cyclists—endurance athletes who exercise continuously for more than 90 minutes. But children should not be taxing their growing bodies to that degree, so they don't really need sports drinks. They need water. It's vitally important to drink fluids before, during, and after sports activity. If a child is more willing to drink a sports drink than water, the sports drink may be worthwhile.

Assist — Statistic credited to fielders when they throw runners out.

Backstop — A high fence behind home plate that protects spectators and keeps batted or thrown balls within the field of play. Also a slang term for the catcher.

Balk — If a pitcher fails to throw the ball to home plate after placing a foot on the pitcher's rubber, the umpire will call a *balk*; all runners then advance one base.

Ball — Any pitch outside the strike zone at which a batter does not swing.

Baselines — Lines extending out from home plate denoting fair and foul territory.

Base runner — Any player who safely reaches base.

Batter — An offensive player who comes up to home plate to try to get on base.

Batter's box — The 6- by 4-foot rectangle on each side of home plate in which batters must stand when they are hitting.

Batting average — The number of hits divided by the number of at-bats; example: A batter with 7 hits in 21 at-bats has a .333 batting average; this is calculated as 7 (hits) divided by 21 (at-bats).

Box score — A detailed summary of statistics from a particular game in box form.

Bunt — A soft hit resulting from the batter holding the bat out and letting the ball hit it instead of swinging the bat.

Catcher — A defensive player who plays behind home plate and receives pitches from the pitcher.

Center fielder — A defensive player that is positioned in the center of the outfield.

Cleanup — The fourth batter in a lineup; there are often runners on base for this batter to drive in and, in that way, "clean up" the bases.

Complete game — A game in which a pitcher pitches every inning.

Cutoff — An infielder who intercepts a throw from an outfielder when runners are on base; the cutoff player then chooses to hold the ball, throw it home, or throw it to a base.

Cycle — A player who has hit a single, double, triple, and home run in one game is said to have hit for the *cycle*.

Diamond — Another word for the infield.

Double — A two-base hit.

Double play — When two outs are made by the defense during one play.

Double steal — A play in which two runners attempt to steal bases at the same time.

Earned run average (ERA) — Calculated as the earned runs multiplied by nine and then divided by the number of innings pitched; example: A pitcher who allows 10 earned runs in 30 innings pitched has an ERA of 3.00; this is calculated as 10 (earned runs) x 9 (innings per game), which equals 90, divided by 30 (innings pitched).

Error — A misplay by a fielder that allows a runner to reach base safely or to score.

Fair territory — Any part of the playing field within the baselines.

First baseman — A defensive player who is positioned on the right side of the infield near first base.

Fly ball — A ball hit high in the air; also called a *popup*.

Force play — A play in which a runner must advance to the next base.

Foul territory — Any part of the playing field outside of the baselines.

Grand slam — A home run with the bases loaded.

Groundball — A ball hit on the ground; also called a *grounder*.

Home plate — A rubber slab at which the batter stands to receive pitches; a batter must start and end a trip around the bases at home plate.

Home run — A four-base hit.

Infield — The part of the field close to home plate that contains the bases; also called a *diamond*.

Infield fly rule — If a batter hits a catchable fly ball above the infield while runners are on first and second or on all three bases with less than two outs, the batter is automatically out; the runners may run to the next base at the risk of being thrown out by a fielder.

GLOSSARY

Inning — A segment of a baseball game in which each team has a turn at bat; major league games are nine innings, while most youth baseball games are six innings.

Left fielder — A defensive player who is positioned on the left side of the outfield.

Line drive — A ball hit in the air straight out from the bat.

Mitt — Another term for a catcher's glove.

No-hitter — A game in which a pitcher or pitchers on the same team do not allow a base hit.

On-base percentage — A batter's number of hits plus walks plus times hit by a pitch divided by the number of at-bats plus walks plus times hit by a pitch.

Outfield — Usually a large, grassy area beyond the infield.

Passed ball — A catchable pitch that gets by the catcher, allowing a base runner to advance; if a passed ball comes on a third strike, the batter can run to first.

Perfect game — A game in which a pitcher pitches every inning and does not let a runner reach base

Pitch — A throw by the pitcher issued to a batter.

Pitcher — A defensive player whose job is to throw the baseball across home plate within the strike zone in an attempt to get the batter out.

Putout — A fielder is credited with a *putout* for catching a fly ball, popup, or line drive, or making a throw that gets an opposing player out; a catcher receives a putout for catching a strikeout

Right fielder — A defensive player who is positioned on the right side of the outfield.

Sacrifice — A bunt or fly ball that allows a runner to score or advance to another base at the expense of the batter, who is out.

Second baseman — A defensive player who is positioned on the right side of the infield near second base.

Shortstop — A defensive player who is positioned on the left side of the infield near second base.

Shutout — A game in which a team loses without scoring.

Single — A one-base hit.

Slugging average — The total number of bases a batter reaches divided by the number of his or her at-bats.

Squeeze play — A play in which a batter attempts to score a runner from third base by bunting the ball.

Stolen base — A base gained by advancing when a batter does not hit a pitch.

Strike — Any pitch that passes through the strike zone; at which a batter swings and misses; or which a batter hits into foul territory.

Strikeout — An out recorded when a pitcher delivers three strikes to a batter during one at-bat.

Strike zone — The area over the plate from the batter's knees up to his or her armpits; if a pitch passes through this area and the batter doesn't swing, the umpire calls a strike.

Tag — To touch a player with the ball for an out.

Tagging up — On a fly ball, waiting until the ball has been caught before leaving a base to advance to the next open base or score a run.

Tee ball league — An organization for youth baseball games in which there is no pitching; the baseball is placed atop a plastic holder, called a *tee*, allowing the hitter to swing the bat at a stationary ball.

Third baseman — A defensive player who is positioned on the left side of the infield near third base.

Triple — A three-base hit.

Walk — A free trip to first base for a batter after a pitcher has issued four balls during one at-bat.

Wild pitch — An erratic, uncatchable pitch that allows a base runner to advance or score. If a wild pitch occurs on a swinging third strike, the batter can run to first base.